People of the Ancient World

THE
ANCIENT
KUSHITES

WRITTEN BY
LIZ SONNEBORN

Franklin Watts
A Division of Scholastic Inc.
New York Toronto London Auckland Sydney
Mexico City New Delhi Hong Kong
Danbury, Connecticut

Note to readers: Definitions for words in bold can be found in the Glossary at the back of this book.

Cover art by Janet Hamlin
Map by XNR Productions Inc.

Photographs © 2005: akg-Images, London: 37, 67, 70, 97; Art Resource, NY: 42, 92 bottom left (Erich Lessing/British Museum, London, UK), 96 bottom (Erich Lessing/Louvre, Paris); Aurora/Gabe Palacio: 86; Bridgeman Art Library International Ltd., London/New York: 72 (Giraudon/Egyptian National Museum, Cairo, Egypt), 79 (Merilyn Thorold); Charles Bonnet/Sudan Archaeological Mission of the University of Geneva: 19, 55, 91 top left; Corbis Images: 50 (Paul Almasy), 68 (Archivo Iconografico, S.A.), 76 (Gianni Dagli Orti), 46, 94 top (Sandro Vannini); Museum of Fine Arts, Boston: 5, 13 (*Cat, 743-712 BC, Marble, Harvard University-Boston Museum of Fine Arts Expedition, 21.305*), 27 (*Earring- Jewelry from tomb of Meroitic Queen, c. 100 BC - 100 AD, gold and enamel, Harvard University-Boston Museum of Fine Arts Expedition, 23.339*), 53 (*Beads and Pendants, c. 593-568 BC, Harvard University-Boston Museum of Fine Arts Expedition, 20.339*), 40 (*Faience horse trappings, c. 712-698 BC, Harvard University-Boston Museum of Fine Arts Expedition, 21.10560*), 43, 92 top, 94 bottom (*Colossal statue of King Aspelta, 593-568 BC, Granite gneiss, Harvard University-Boston Museum of Fine Arts Expedition, 23.730*), 24 (*Statue of Senkamanisken, 643-623 BC, Granodiorite gneiss, Harvard University-Boston Museum of Fine Arts Expedition, 23.731*), 32 (*Stele of King Tanyidamani, 160-180 AD, Granite gneiss, Harvard University-Boston Museum of Fine Arts Expedition, 23.736*), 60 (*Statue of Khonsouiraa, c. 760-660 BC, Black diorite, James Fund and Contribution, 07.494*), 17 (*Stela of the Nubian soldier Nenu, 2100-2040 BC, painted limestone, Purchased by A.M. Lythgoe, 03.1848*); The Art Archive/Picture Desk: 38, 64, 81 (Dagli Orti/Egyptian Museum, Cairo), 14, 90 top (Dagli Orti/Egyptian Museum, Turin), 85 (Dagli Orti/Private Collection), 83 (Dagli Orti/San Vitale Ravenna, Italy), 57 (Staatliche Sammlung Agyptischer Kunst, Munich); The Image Works: 29 (The British Museum/Topham-HIP), 25, 96 top (Jeff Moore/PressNet/Topham), 12, 90 bottom (Photri/Topham), 75 (Topham); Timothy Kendall: 9, 28, 47, 58, 88, 91 top right; University of Pennslyvania Museum: 62 (E8183); Woodfin Camp & Associates/Mike Yamashita; 4 center, 7, 48, 73, 78 top left, 92 bottom right; Worcester Art Museum, Worcester, Massachusetts: 35 (Museum purchase, 1922.145P).

Library of Congress Cataloging-in-Publication Data

Sonneborn, Liz.
    The ancient Kushites / Liz Sonneborn.
    p. cm. — (People of the ancient world)

Includes bibliographical references and index.
ISBN 0-531-12380-4 (lib. bdg.)   0-531-16847-6 (pbk.)
1. Cushites—Juvenile literature. I. Title. II. Series.
DT367.45.C86S65 2005
939'.78—dc22

                              2004013908

Contents

STUDYING THE KUSHITES

IN THE SUMMER OF 1905, ARCHAEOLOGIST James Henry Breasted began a six-month trek across the African desert. Accompanying him were two fellow scientists, his wife Frances, and his eight-year-old son Charles. Traveling through sandstorms and insect swarms, they made their way deep into the lands south of Egypt. Finally, the expedition came upon the ruins of great temples and pyramids built thousands of years earlier.

Breasted set to work. He took many photographs at several sites, including Meroë, Naqa, and Muswwarates-Sufra. These images created an astounding record of an ancient culture that was then all but unknown. Breasted's expedition and those of other archaeologists who followed him introduced the world to the mighty kingdom of **Kush**, one of the world's greatest ancient civilizations.

For more than one thousand years, Kush was a powerful force in what is present-day Africa. It was ruled by kings and queens who built enormous temples and tombs to glorify themselves and their gods. The Kushites developed a written language and created some of the ancient world's finest pottery and metalwork. The people of Kush also played an instrumental role in an early trade network that stretched across what is now southeastern Asia and northern Africa.

What Was Kush?

The word "Kush" was first used in about 1550 B.C. It was the name the Egyptians gave to the land along the Nile River directly to the south of their territory. The area later became known as **Nubia**. That name came from the Noba or Nuba, a people who occupied the Nile Valley after the Kushite civilization had collapsed. Kush is also known as "Cush."

Today, scholars of the ancient world sometime use the words "Nubia" and "Kush" interchangeably. In modern Africa, however, "Nubia" more often refers to the lands of the Nubians, an ethnic group descended from the Noba people of long ago.

In this book "Nubia" will be used as archaeologists use it today. It will describe the lands of the Nile River valley south of the city of Aswan in southern Egypt and north of the city of Khartoum in central Sudan. "Kush" will refer to the ancient kingdom centered in southern Nubia that flourished from about 800 B.C. to about A.D. 360.

The Unknown Kingdom

Kush was one of two great ancient civilizations of Africa. The other was its northern neighbor, Egypt. Famed as the land of pyramids and pharaohs, Egypt has been studied exhaustively by historians and archaeologists. But Kush was largely ignored by scholars until fairly recently.

There are several reasons for this. One is that the Egyptians left behind descriptions of their beliefs, customs, and history using a system of picture writing called **hieroglyphs**. They carved these symbols onto stone slabs called **stelae** and painted them in books made of papyrus, a paper-like material.

The Kushites also had their own writing system. It is known as **Meroitic** after the kingdom's last capital, Meroë. Meroitic, however, gives scholars far less information than Egyptian hieroglyphic writing does. Meroitic was used in Kush for a relatively short period—from about 180 B.C. to A.D. 400, only about half of the kingdom's history. But, worse for students of Kush, no one today knows how to read Meroitic. Scholars are able to recognize only a few names of places and people.

As a result, descriptions of Kush written by the Kushites themselves

This stele, showing Meroitic writing, was placed in a tomb. The figure is a depiction of the deceased.

are hard to come by. There are just a few tomb **inscriptions** written in hieroglyphs dating from the kingdom's early years. Unfortunately, their focus is fairly limited. They record some information about the Kushite religion and military victories but say little about the people's culture or thought.

In Others' Words

Luckily, there are other records about Kush. These were written by various peoples who came in contact with the Kushites. Many came from Egypt, because the history of the Egyptians and the Kushites were deeply intertwined. But Egyptian evaluations of Kushite culture are hardly objective. For many centuries, Egypt and Kush fought for control of the Nile River valley. Often, they were at war. As a result, Egyptian writings usually regard the Kushites at best with suspicion and at worst with contempt.

For instance, inscriptions on Egyptian tombs tend to be insulting to the Kushites. Because the inscriptions are meant to glorify the entombed kings, they emphasize the Egyptians' military conquests and often insult the Kushites, their enemies. Kush itself is often called "miserable" or "wretched."

Writers from ancient Greece and Rome also contribute to our understanding of the Kushites. Similar to Egyptian sources, these documents offer limited insight into the Kushite way of life. Only a few Greeks and Romans actually traveled to Kush. These writers, therefore, tended to regard the Kushites as strange, mysterious people, important largely for the roles they played in Egyptian history and in trade. For these ancient writers the dark skin of the Kushites added to their exoticism. They referred to the Kushites as Aithiopians (also spelled "Ethiopians"), after a Greek word meaning "burnt-faced people."

Digging for Information

With so few written sources available, scholars largely shape their vision of Kush through **archaeology**. Archaeologists reconstruct the lives of ancient peoples by excavating (digging up) sites where they lived and by studying the objects they left behind. These artifacts include houses, graves, tools, weapons, pottery, and other **artifacts**.

Unfortunately, the archaeological record of Kush remains sketchy. Over the centuries, many sites were destroyed by erosion or buried under desert silt and sand. Others were looted by fortune hunters. Adding to the problem, relatively few Kushite sites have been fully excavated. Starting in the nineteenth century, adventurers traveled to Nubia and wrote about the Kushite ruins they saw. American and European archaeologists, however, preferred to perform **excavations** of ancient Egyptian sites.

There was probably an element of racism in their preference. Many white archaeologists of that time regarded the dark-skinned people of Kush as less worthy of study than the lighter-skinned Egyptians. Those archaeologists who did take an interest in Nubian sites were Egyptologists. They studied Kush largely for what it could

Archaeologists uncover an ancient living room in a private house, dating back to 400 B.C.–200 B.C.

tell them about Egyptian history. Fascinated with the ancient Egyptians, they were prone to dismiss the Kushite civilization as an inferior copy of ancient Egyptian culture. Even when presented with impressive artifacts from Kush, some archaeologists struggled to find explanations that would prove they could not have been made by the dark-skinned Kushites. Characteristic of these efforts, American travel writer Bayard Taylor concluded in the 1850s, without any evidence, that the Kushites (as well as the Egyptians) could not possibly have been black: "The sculptures at [Meroë] . . . establish the important fact that the ancient Ethiopians, though of a darker complexion than the Egyptians (as they are, in fact, represented in Egyptian sculpture), were, like them, an offshoot of the great Caucasian [white] race."

In part because of such racist views, extensive archaeological excavation of Kushite sites did not begin until the mid-twentieth century. Since then, teams of archaeologists have worked to salvage long-forgotten artifacts. Through their efforts, the study of Kush has been revolutionized, allowing scholars at last to reconstruct one of the greatest civilizations of the ancient world.

Chapter I

THE EARLY NUBIANS

According to current archaeological research, humans had established large, permanent settlements in Nubia by about 6000 B.C.—more than five thousand years before the rise of Kush. Tools found at sites from this period show that the early Nubians knew how to grow grain and raise domesticated animals. The lives of these Nubians was dictated by the Nile River, which flowed from the south to the north through their lands. This 1,000-mile (1,609-kilometer) stretch of river created a long strip of habitable land through the vast desert that extended across what is now northern Africa.

On the Nile

In Egypt the great river flooded annually, spreading a layer of fertile silt that proved ideal for farming. In Nubia, however, the floods were less extensive. As a result, Nubia had less farmable land and could sustain fewer people than Egypt. The population of ancient Nubia, therefore, was always much smaller than that of ancient Egypt.

The river also took a far different course in Nubia than it did in Egypt. In Egypt the Nile was fairly straight. But south of Aswan,

From an aerial photograph, it is possible to see the course of the Nile River.

Nubian Cats

Nubia might have been the first home of the domestic cat. According to one theory, cats were present in Nubia by about 3000 B.C. About five hundred years later they had been exported to Egypt. In time Egyptians began worshipping the cat as a goddess. Because of its sacred status, killing a cat was an offense punishable by death. It was also illegal to export cats. When Egyptian soldiers found a cat in foreign lands, they made a point of taking it back with them, since Egypt was regarded as the cat's real home. In keeping with cats' high regard in Egyptian society, Egyptian artists often honored cats by depicting them in sculpture and jewelry.

the river snaked in a giant S-shape through Nubia's center. In Nubia the river's flow was interrupted by a series of six areas where rocks and islands created rapids in the water. These areas are known as **cataracts**. The cataracts, combined with the river's winding course, made it difficult to travel through Nubia by boat.

Precious Diorite

In the eyes of the early Egyptians, one of Nubia's most precious resources was **diorite**, a dark bluish stone. Pharaohs sent teams of laborers to Nubia to mine this treasure. Using ropes, workers pulled blocks of diorite weighing many tons across the desert before loading them into ships on the Nile. In Egypt diorite was carved into statues and used to decorate the interior chambers of the pharaohs' pyramids.

Most people in Nubia lived close to the Nile. To the north, where there was almost no rainfall, it was nearly impossible to survive any distance away from the river. The surrounding land was so dry that it could barely sustain human life. In the southern stretches of Nubia, however, there was a rain belt. The semideserts there had enough water to sustain a limited number of people and animals and fairly hardy vegetation. The people who inhabited these lands were **nomads**. They moved with the seasons to places where they could hunt animals and gather wild plants.

The A-Group and the C-Group

Graves excavated in northern Nubia show that by about 3500 B.C. the Nubians had developed a more advanced culture. A variety of objects were found inside graves, including food jars, copper tools, and other luxury goods from Egypt. These artifacts suggest that Nubians at that time, referred to as the A-Group by archaeologists, had established themselves as the middlemen in a vast trade network. With their territory situated between Egypt and what is now central Africa, the A-Group Nubians could control the trade between peoples to the north and those to the south. They may have obtained the Egyptian grave goods through trade or as payment for allowing Egyptian traders to travel up the Nile.

In about 3100 B.C., the people of Egypt were united under one ruler, called a pharaoh. Probably wanting to dominate trade along the whole length of the Nile, the early pharaohs became determined to conquer Nubia. Their warriors repeatedly invaded Nubia, eventually taking control of Nubian land north of the Second Cataract. The A-Group Nubians in the area were either driven into the desert or assimilated into the Egyptian population.

Qustul

In the early 1960s, a team of archaeologists excavated the A-Group-era site of Qustul, located about 180 miles (290 km) up the Nile from Aswan. They uncovered a series of tombs filled with Egyptian trade goods. In the 1980s, Bruce B. Williams of the Oriental Institute at the University of Chicago began studying these objects. He was especially intrigued by two incense burn- ers, made from sandstone from Nubia and decorated with images of kings. Williams main- tained that they were early kings of Nubia, though his the- ory contradicted the prevailing belief that Nubia at that time was not yet organized under a single ruler. If Williams's contro- versial theory is correct, African kingship originated in Nubia, rather than in Egypt, as it is commonly thought today.

The Egyptians held on to northern Nubia for several hundred years, until attacks by desert tribes forced them to retreat from the area. Nubians, known to archaeologists as the C-Group, then returned to their northern territory. The C-Group Nubians even- tually resumed trade with Egypt, supplying wood for building projects and stones for the pharaohs' pyramids. The Egyptians also began hiring Nubian warriors to serve in their army.

Kerma Culture

By about 2000 B.C., Egypt succeeded in reoccupying northern Nubia. It established a series of forts all the way south to the Sec- ond Cataract. The forts provided protection for traders. But they

Some members of the C-Group Nubians served as soldiers in the Egyptian army.
A stele shows a Nubian soldier named Nenu with his Egyptian wife.

Harkhuf in Nubia

One of the most important written sources about early Nubia is an inscription discovered in the tomb of Harkhuf, who served as an Egyptian official around 2300 B.C. On the order of the pharaoh, he led several trading expeditions into Nubia. His caravan of three hundred donkeys carried back home many foreign products, including ivory, ebony, leopard skins, and ostrich feathers. Harkhuf wisely hired an army of Nubians to guard his precious cargo and make sure it arrived safely into the pharaoh's hands.

were also meant to deal with the gathering threat to the south, as the Nubians were becoming more politically unified. These people's main settlement was just south of the Third Cataract at the site of the present-day Sudanese village of Kerma. The settlement at Kerma became the first true urban center of Nubia. Because of the concentration of people and power there, scholars sometimes call Kerma the first kingdom of Kush.

The Nubian settlement at Kerma included a palace, a religious center, and about two hundred houses, all surrounded by stone walls and moats to keep out intruders. Outside the walls were many more houses and small temples. A few miles away was a vast cemetery that contained about thirty thousand graves. Most were covered with mounds ringed with pebbles, but those entombing Kerma's rulers were far grander. Royal burial mounds were about 300 feet (91 meters) in diameter and contained an internal burial chamber filled with the deceased's most prized possessions.

A Swiss team of archaeologists excavate the early Nubian city of Kerma.

As Kerma grew more powerful, the Egyptian pharaohs became weaker. They fell prey to the Hyksos, a people from the north who set out to conquer Egypt. The Hyksos king sent a letter to the ruler of Kerma. It suggested a plot. The Nubians could attack Egypt from the south, the Hyksos could attack it from the north, and once Egypt was defeated, the Hyksos and the Nubians could split its territory.

The Egyptian pharaoh Kamose intercepted the message, foiling the plan. After he and his successor, Ahmose, drove off the Hyksos, they turned their attention to Nubia, a growing power they no longer trusted. In about 1500 B.C., the Egyptians invaded. They destroyed Kerma and eventually established control over Nubian lands all the way south to the Fifth Cataract.

The Emergence of Kush

With the taking of Nubia, Egypt became the wealthiest kingdom in the world. The pharaohs required the Nubians to pay them tribute, which included such goods as cattle, ivory, and slaves. But

Kerma Burial Customs

The way the dead were buried at Kerma was unique in the ancient world. Corpses were placed in oval or round pits, about 5 feet (1.5 meters) deep, and surrounded by the dead's possessions. The bodies were always twisted into the same position. They were laid on their right side on a hide or, later, a bed made of wood. Their feet were moved toward the west, and their heads toward the east. The hands of the dead were placed over their faces before the burial pits were filled in.

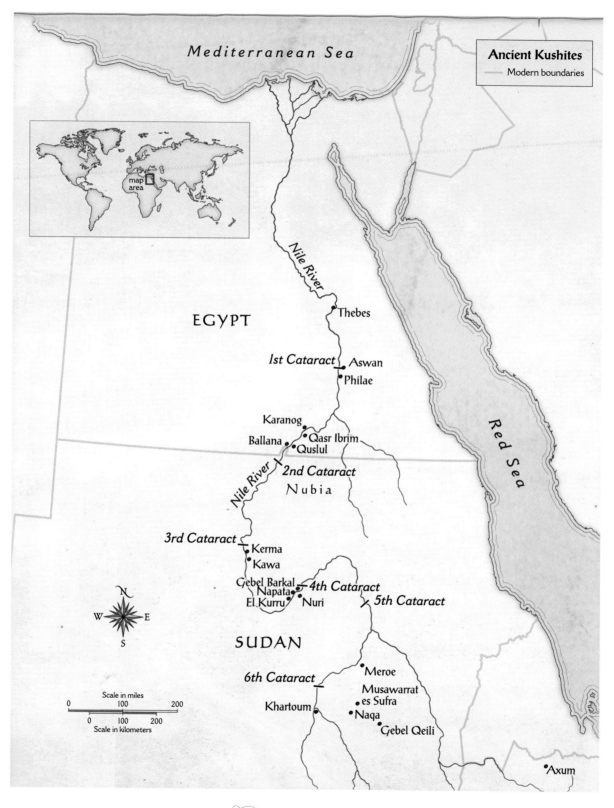

Mediterranean Sea

Ancient Kushites
— Modern boundaries

map area

Nile River

EGYPT

Thebes

1st Cataract • Aswan
• Philae

Karanog •
• Qasr Ibrim
Ballana • • Quslul

Nile River

2nd Cataract
N u b i a

Red Sea

3rd Cataract • Kerma
• Kawa

Gebel Barkal • *4th Cataract*
Napata •
El Kurru • • Nuri
5th Cataract

N
W E
S

SUDAN

6th Cataract • Meroe

Musawarrat
es Sufra
Khartoum • • Naqa

Gebel Qeili

• Axum

Scale in miles
0   100   200

0   100   200
Scale in kilometers

most of all, the pharaohs wanted Nubian gold. They used gold to create beautiful objects to glorify themselves. Many of the treasures from the tomb of Egyptian pharaoh Tutankhamen are made from Nubian gold. The metal also played an important role in the Egyptians dealings with other peoples because Egypt's leaders offered gold as gifts to foreign diplomats.

The Egyptians did not dominate Nubia for long. By about 1100 B.C., they had retreated, probably because internal political troubles in Egypt made it impossible for the pharaohs to concentrate on holding Nubian lands. Almost nothing is known about Nubia during the next three hundred years. Egyptian sources are silent about this period, probably because the pharaohs' failure to retain Nubia was considered an embarrassment. By about 800 B.C., however, a new urban center known as Napata began to grow near the Fourth Cataract. There, the Nubians, like the Egyptians, were united under the rule of a line of powerful kings. The stage was set for the emergence of one of the greatest empires of ancient times, the kingdom of Kush.

Chapter II

KINGS AND QUEENS

Writing in the first century B.C., the ancient Greek historian Diodorus described the elaborate coronation ceremony that marked the transfer of power to a new Kushite king: "[The king] is carried about in accordance with a certain custom during a festival. . . . The people then immediately prostrate themselves and honor him like a god on the ground that the rule had been entrusted to him by divine providence."

Though considered godlike by his followers, the new king was not free to do whatever he chose. Instead, Diodorus explained, "the person so chosen follows a way of life determined by the laws, and in other matters acts in accordance with ancestral custom." By observing these old ways, the king assured the Kushites that they were wise to place their faith in his rule.

Taking the Throne

It is unclear how the class of kings first emerged in Kush. But just before Kush became a kingdom (c. 800 B.C.), Nubia was controlled by the Egyptian pharaohs. To oversee the day-to-day governing of Nubia, the pharaohs appointed an official, called the

While their people treated them like gods, Kushite kings could not do as they pleased, because they were expected to follow certain traditions.

"viceroy of Kush." These viceroys were possibly Nubians. The first kings could have come from the families of the old viceroys.

Exactly how the Kushites chose a new ruler when a king died is also not entirely clear. The subject fascinated ancient writers, though. The Greek historian Herodotus believed that a new Kushite king was "the man among the citizens whom they find to be the tallest and to have strength in proportion to his height." Nicolaus of Damascus said that the kingship fell to one of the sons of the dead king's sister. If there were no sons, the Kushites chose "as king the most handsome of all and most warlike." Another Greek writer, Strabo, held that "they appoint as kings those who are distinguished by beauty or skill in cattle-breeding or courage or wealth."

More likely, a ruler was selected from a pool of candidates related to the deceased king. The new king was often the brother or nephew of the old one, but not always. In a few cases, a female relative was selected to serve as queen. Some queens may have been the wives of former rulers. At least one shared

power with her husband. Queen Amanitore and King Natakamani were joint rulers during the first century A.D. On Kushite art,
they are pictured together in identical poses as a symbol of their
equal status.

In many cases, priests made the final decision about who
would succeed a deceased king. The Kushites believed the priests'

**Queen Amanitore and King Natakamani are showed here holding up the sky on
this part of a temple for Isis found in upper Nubia.**

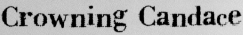

Crowning Candace

Several Roman writers identified female rulers of Kush as "Kandake" (pronounced kan-DAH-key). In fact, this was not a name but a title. The Meroitic word probably meant "queen" or "mother of the prince." The girl's name Candace comes from this ancient word from the Kushite civilization.

choice was guided by Amun, an Egyptian god that also became the most important god to the people of Kush. Some inscriptions, however, suggest that, in particularly desperate times, the army stepped in to pick the royal successor.

This happened in 430 B.C., when Irike-amanote took the throne. When the previous king died, there was no obvious successor. A desert tribe took advantage of Kush's political confusion and staged an attack. Afraid the situation was getting out of hand, army leaders moved quickly to put Irike-amanote into power. He then led a successful campaign against the desert peoples.

Looking Royal

Many Kushite sculptures and paintings depict the ceremonial clothing of Kush's royals. A king was often dressed in a white robe, sometimes with a red shawl tossed over the right shoulder. Others wore a knee-length skirt, perhaps part of a war costume. In one depiction, a king appears in body armor to celebrate his role as the leader of Kush's army. Both kings and queens wore heavy jewelry, including earrings, necklaces, and armlets.

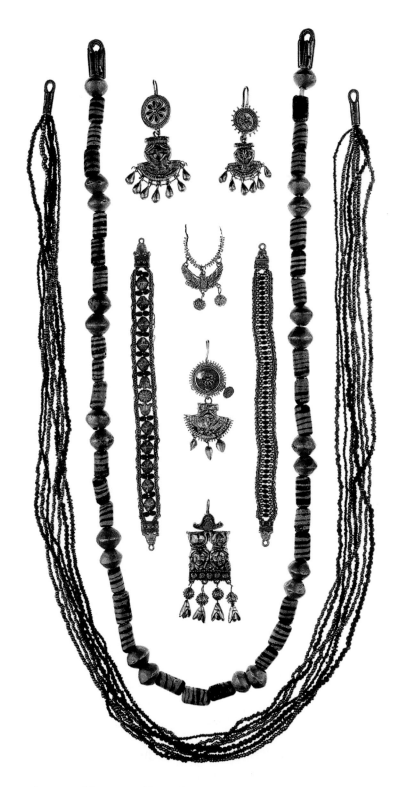

These earrings, necklaces, and bracelets were worn by a Kushite queen sometime between 100 B.C. to A.D. 100.

A wall painting shows a figure wearing one of the most common forms of crowns in ancient Kush. It was adorned with uraei—two sacred serpents that symbolized the Kushite kingship.

Royal headgear was even more varied. Kushite artists depicted more than twenty different types of crowns. Some were modeled after those worn by the Egyptian pharaohs. One type of crown particularly prevalent in Kush was made from a cap of metal or leather with two sacred serpents, called **uraei**, uncoiling from it. The uraei were thought to protect the king from harm. Diodorus believed they were "a sign that those who dare to attack the king will meet with fatal bites."

The Inner Circle

Rulers were also protected by a circle of close associates. These people were expected to be unfailingly loyal. If a king lost a foot, his friends had to cut off one of their own. As Diodorus wrote, "They believe that it would be shameful if the king was lame and his friends were sound of foot."

When a ruler died, his associates were also expected to commit suicide. Because of this custom, a ruler's friends were careful to protect him from any harm. According to Diodorus, "[I]t is for this reason . . . that a conspiracy against the king is not easily raised among the [Kushites], all his friends being equally concerned both for his safety and their own."

The ruler of Kush was also assisted by relatives who served as members of the court. Some were placed in charge of the Kushite army. Before becoming a king himself in 690 B.C., Taharqa was sent to battle invading Assyrians by the king Shebitqo, who was probably Taharqa's older brother. Other relatives became the ruler's representatives in outlying

King Taharqa is being protected by the god Amun who is shown here in the form of a ram. This statue was found at a temple in present-day Sudan and dates back to 690 B.C.–664 B.C.

Law and Order

The ancient Greek historian Diodorus wrote of how the kings of Kush condemned criminals to death. Instead of ordering an execution, a king sent "one of his servants bearing a symbol of death to the criminal. He upon seeing the symbol, immediately [went] to his own house and [killed] himself." According to Diodorus, one criminal refused to commit suicide and prepared to flee. But before he could get away, the criminal's mother murdered him to keep him from bringing further shame to the family.

areas of the empire. King Aspelta, for instance, sent his sons far from the capital to serve as administrators.

Royal Duties

The king had plenty of responsibilities of his own. At times, especially during the period when Kush controlled Egypt (747 B.C.–656 B.C.), the Kushite kings had power over an extensive territory. Protecting it from invaders was a constant struggle. Kush's ruler had to be prepared to battle both neighboring desert tribes and foreign invaders. The king's role as a military leader was so important that, at least in several cases, a candidate for the kingship was chosen over other potential rulers because he had proved himself on the battlefield.

Oftentimes, rulers of Kush had to be diplomats. In A.D. 60, for instance, a Kushite queen met with representatives of the Roman emperor Nero. They had been sent to explore Kush, possibly to determine it if could be conquered by Roman troops. The queen, even if she suspected their motives, greeted the explorers

Gifts from a Queen

The Alexander Romance, a collection of stories written in the third century B.C. about Alexander the Great, includes an imagined letter from a Kushite queen, chronicling the exotic gifts she sent to curry favor with this powerful Macedonian (Greek) leader: "My ambassadors are bringing you 100 ingots of solid gold, 500 Aithiopian [Ethiopian] youths, 200 parrots, 200 apes, and for our god Amun . . . a crown of emeralds and unpierced pearls, 10 chains bearing seals and 80 ivory caskets. The species of wild beasts sent by us are 350 elephants, 300 leopards, 80 rhinoceroses, 4 panthers, 90 man-eating dogs in cages, 300 fighting bulls, 90 elephant tusks, 300 leopard skins, 1500 shafts of ebony. Send at once whom you want to pick up these gifts, and write to us when you have conquered the world."

graciously. She also gave them letters of introduction to important leaders in the south. Perhaps, with the letters, she wanted to show that the Kushites had cultivated good relationships with peoples in interior Africa in hopes of discouraging a Roman invasion. The Roman expedition eventually returned home and reported that an invasion of Kush would not be worth the trouble.

Kushite rulers were also religious leaders. Scholars disagree over whether the Kushites considered their kings and queens to be gods and goddesses. But it is clear that the people of Kush were convinced their rulers were given their power to rule from the god Amun. Kushite rulers were also responsible for overseeing

King Tanyidamani honors the lion god Apedemak. The Kushites believed that their rulers received their power from the gods.

the work of priests. These holy men made sure religious ceremonies were properly conducted and temples were well maintained.

Many rulers devoted time to grand building projects. They ordered the construction of lavish palaces for themselves as well as the building of new temples and the rebuilding of old ones that had fallen into disrepair. As monuments to their own personal glory, these buildings were especially important for rulers who had not been the clear choice to succeed the previous king. These projects helped celebrate both a king's greatness and his **piety**, confirming to the people of Kush that he was the true and proper ruler in Amun's eyes.

Chapter III

WARRIORS

The tomb inscription of Piankhy, perhaps Kush's greatest warrior king, issues a warning to the kingdom's warriors: "Boast not to the lord of might, for the brave has no might without him. He makes the weak-armed strong-armed, so that many may lie before the few, and a single one conquers a thousand men!" Piankhy was reminding his army that their power came from the great god Amun. But Piankhy also emphasized that with Amun on their side, there was no foe the warriors could not conquer.

Publicly, the kings of Kush also hailed Amun as the source of their power. In truth, however, they could not have maintained their positions without the help of the warriors in their service. With its large territory and small population, Kush was hard to protect against intruders, especially along the edges of the kingdom. Surrounded by potential enemies, the Kushite kings had to rely on their army just to keep the kingdom intact. But for a few kings in the sixth and seventh centuries B.C., the army did far more. The kingdom's fighting force allowed them to take advantage of the weaknesses of the pharaohs to the north and to claim Egypt as their own.

The Army

Little is known about the makeup of the Kushite army. It may have been a professional fighting force, or it may have

This sandstone carving shows a prince about to slay his enemies. The symbol of victory floats behind him. Kushite leaders relied on their armies to maintain their power.

been a **militia**, called up for service only in times of emergency. Probably there was at least a small permanent army charged with protecting the king.

The Greek historian Herodotus left a description of the clothing and weapons of the Kushite soldier: "The Ethiopians [Kushites] were clothed in panthers' and lions' skins, and carried long bows, not less than four cubits [6 feet or 2 meters] in length, made from branches of palm trees, and on them they placed short arrows made of cane." He also noted that they carried clubs and javelins with tips made from antelope horn. When the Kushites headed into battle, Herodotus further noted, "they smeared one half of their body with chalk, and the other half with red [pigment]."

The Greek writer Strabo claimed the Kushite soldiers were poorly armed. Yet he wrote that they had **pikes**, swords, bows, and hatchets. Most also carried large shields made of animal hides. In some Kushite artwork, rulers are shown wearing body armor, but foot soldiers probably had no such protection. Kings, queens, and gods are also pictured wearing large stone rings. Smaller versions have been found on the thumbs of skeletons in Kushite graves. The stone rings were worn by bowmen so they could pull back a bowstring without cutting their hands.

According to Herodotus, the Kushites tipped their arrows with stone points "on which they engrave seals." At sites in Kush, archaeologists have found many stone arrowheads and a few made from metal. In some graves, they have uncovered clusters of iron-headed arrows with one copper-headed arrow mixed in. Archaeologists speculate that warriors thought the copper arrowhead had the magical power to make the iron arrowheads more deadly.

Warriors generally stored their stone-tipped arrows in leather quivers. The iron- and copper-tipped ones, however, were kept in

An Egyptian wall carving shows Kushite soldiers carrying long bows and hatchets.

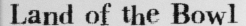

Land of the Bowl

In the ancient world, the Kushites were famed for their archery skills. Before the emergence of the kingdom of Kush, Egypt routinely hired thousands of Nubian archers to beef up its army. Early Egyptian inscriptions refer to Nubia as "the land of the bow." In hieroglyphs, Nubia was represented first as a bow above a strip of land and later as a bow above a conquered enemy.

special quivers made from copper with bells attached. The extra protection of the copper quivers and a strange discoloration on many of the metal arrowheads suggest that these were poisoned arrows.

Elephants and Horses

The warriors of Kush possibly were the first people in the ancient world to ride into battle on elephants. Kushite traders also provided war elephants for the Egyptian army. The important role elephants played in warfare in ancient Africa is clear from their many depictions in art. One of the most famous is a Kushite carving on the wall of the Lion Temple at Muswwarat es-Sufra, which shows a row of elephants leading a group of bound prisoners.

In about 1700 B.C., the Hyksos brought horses to Egypt, and soon afterward they were introduced to Nubia. By the Kushite era, the Kushites were known as great horse trainers. Foreign rulers often hired horsemen from Kush to care for their private herds.

The kings of Kush were especially proud of their horses. At the temple of Amun at the sacred site of Jebel Barkal, several walls are illustrated with processions of stately horses, gifts from Egyptian pharaohs to Kushite royals. Sometimes, a king's horses were buried with him. The bodies of the animals were placed in a standing position in graves deep enough to hold them up to the neck. Their heads were then covered with dirt to form small mounds.

King Piankhy was particularly fond of horses. According to an inscription at Jebel Barkal, while he was waging war on Egypt, he found a horse herd belonging to an Egyptian prince and "perceived that they had been suffering from hunger." The king was horrified by the condition of the horse stables. He declared, "I

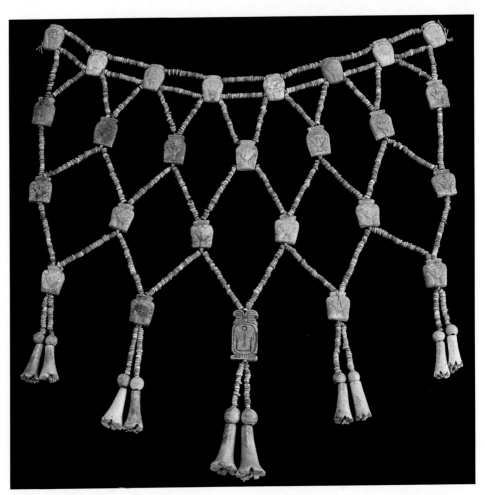

Horses were important to the Kushites. This item is part of a decoration that a horse would wear around its neck.

swear by my own life . . . that to my mind to have allowed my horses to suffer is the worst of all the evil things which thou hast done."

Victory Over Egypt

The inscriptions on the tombs of Kushite kings understandably celebrate the kingdom's military power. But written sources left behind by Kush's enemies are generally dismissive of the kingdom's army. For instance, an inscription on a rock erected by the Egyptians along the Egyptian-Nubian border declared their contempt for the typical Nubian fighter: "Attack him, he will turn his back; retreat, he will start attacking. They are not people one respects; they are wretches, craven-hearted [cowardly]." Still, there is one piece of evidence that suggests the warriors of Kush were more formidable than their enemies wanted to admit. They succeeded in protecting the Kush kingdom from outsiders for more than one thousand years.

Kush's army was perhaps at its most powerful between 747 B.C. and 656 B.C. During these years, the Kushite kings not only controlled Nubia but also ruled Egypt as the pharaohs of the Twenty-Fifth **Dynasty**. Their empire was the largest ever created in ancient Africa.

Several early Kushite rulers invaded Egypt before King Piankhy finally conquered Kush's northern neighbor, becoming the first pharaoh of the Twenty-Fifth Dynasty. At the time, several Egyptian princes were fighting each other for power over Egypt. With the Egyptian leadership divided, Piankhy's warriors were able to defeat the Egyptian army in a series of skirmishes. Piankhy claimed the kingship of both Egypt and Kush, declaring that his victory was Amun's will. Piankhy then returned to the Kushite capital of Napata from which he continued to rule over Egypt.

With Piankhy's death, princes in northern Egypt saw an opportunity to retake their land. They rebelled against Kushite rule, forcing Shabaqo, Piankhy's successor, to lead the army back into Egypt. Again, the Kushites overtook the enemy. Realizing that he could never keep his hold on Egypt if he lived in faraway Napata, Shabaqo became the first Kushite king to live in Egypt. He and his successor Taharqa became immersed in Egyptian culture. During their reigns, many Egyptian customs, building techniques, and art styles were introduced to Kush.

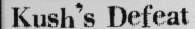

Kush's Defeat

In the Bible, the story of the Assyrians' victory over the Kushites is presented as a cautionary tale for anyone with the arrogance to believe he or she is indestructible. In Nahum 3:8–10, the prophet Nahum wrote, "Are you better than [the Egyptian city of] Thebes that sat by the Nile, with water around her, her rampart a sea, and water her wall? Ethiopia [Kush] was her strength, Egypt, too, and that without limit. . . . Yet she was carried away, . . . and her great men were bound in chains."

Losing an Empire

Kushite rule over Egypt soon faced a new threat. When Taharqa was king, Egypt was invaded by warriors from Assyria, a kingdom in what is now Iraq. The Assyrian king described the clash between the Kushite and Assyrian armies: "Tarku [Taharqa], king of Egypt and Kush, heard of the advance of my army and mustered his fighting men against me, offering armed resistance and battle. . . . I defeated his army in a battle on the open plain. Tarku heard of the defeat of his armies, while in Memphis. . . . He forsook Memphis and fled to save his life."

Tanwetamani, Taharqa's nephew, became the next king in 664 B.C. According to a stele inscription, Tanwetamani had a dream in which he saw two snakes. Interpreting the dream to mean he would rule both Kush and Egypt, he again sent the Kushite army to reclaim Egypt. The force secured Egypt, but Kush was able to hold on it for only two years. The Assyrians resumed their attacks, and Tanwetamani fled. Kush's army was too weak to continue the fight for Egypt. With Tanwetamani's reign, Kush lost control of Egypt forever.

In 593 B.C., the Egyptians took their revenge. Under the orders of the pharaoh Psammeticus II, the Egyptian army marched deep into the heart of Kush. They destroyed Napata, forcing King Aspelta to flee. When Aspelta's palace at Napata was excavated in 1996, archaeologists found statues of several Kushite kings that had been broken into pieces, possibly by angry Egyptian troops. After the Egyptian invasion, the capital of Kush was moved south to Meroë.

King Aspelta forced to leave Napata after the Egyptians attacked in 593 B.C. Kushites created a new capital city in Meroë.

New Enemies

Egypt soon faced new and formidable enemies. The kingdom was overtaken first by the Persians and then by the Greeks, led by Alexander the Great. Alexander installed his general Ptolemy as Egypt's new ruler. During this tumultuous period, Kush remained independent.

In 33 B.C., the Ptolemaic queen, Cleopatra, was defeated by the Romans, and Egypt became a Roman province. Almost immediately, the leaders of Rome began eyeing Kush and its wealth. When they attempted to levy taxes on the people of northern Kush, the Kushites revolted. The Romans sent an army into Kush to put down the rebellion. The fighting ended with the Treaty of Samos. Negotiated by the ambassadors of a Kushite queen (probably Amanishakheto), the Romans agreed to withdraw from most of Kush. They only retained control over the Dodecaschoenus, a 70-mile (113-km) area along the Nile in northern Kush.

The treaty ushered in a golden age in Kush during which increased trade with the Romans helped the economy to flourish. Egypt, its greatest rival, had fallen to foreign powers. But, with the help of its warrior class, Kush had been able to retain its independence. Free from domination by its enemies, Kush continued to grow and prosper for the next three hundred years.

Chapter IV

PRIESTS

"Historians . . . say that the honoring of gods and the conducting of sacrifices, processions, festivals, and other ways by which men worship the divine first were introduced among the Aithiopians [Kushites]. For this reason their piety has become famous among all men, and the sacrifices performed by the Aithiopians are believed to be particularly agreeable to the divine power."

The Greek historian Diodorus wrote this description of the Kushites in the first century B.C. As his account attests, the Kushites were renowned throughout the ancient world for their piety—their religious devotion and reverence for their gods.

Priests and Kings

The Kushites' religious life was overseen by a class of priests. These priests managed temples throughout the kingdom. They also wielded considerable political power. Close relatives of the king were often appointed to the priesthood. When Kush controlled Egypt, a particularly powerful position was the high priestess of Thebes. Revealing the importance of this position, the priestess was called the wife of the god Amun.

As interpreters of Amun's wishes, the priests also had great influence over the rulers of Kush. In addition to helping choose successors to the kingship, priests instructed ruling kings on important matters of state. Because the priests' counsel was

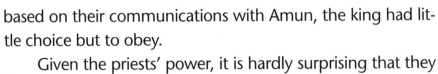

based on their communications with Amun, the king had little choice but to obey.

Given the priests' power, it is hardly surprising that they sometimes clashed with the royals. At the religious center of Jebel Barkal, for instance, the name of King Aspelta was scratched off two stelae, possibly because he angered the priests there. Another stele tells the story of a king, perhaps Aspelta, who forbade a group of priests to enter a temple. The king believed they planned to kill a man even though Amun had not demanded his execution. Although the meaning of the inscription is not entirely clear, the priests might have been plotting to kill the king himself.

Arkamani-qo's Revenge

According to Diodorus, the priests had the power to order the death of a king. In what he called "the strangest of all their customs," the priests sometimes sent messengers to a king to inform him it was time to die. Because the priests held that this demand came Amun, the king was obliged to commit suicide. As Diodorus wrote, "The kings obeyed the priests, not having been conquered by weapons or force but their reason having been overcome by this superstition."

Diodorus added that this practice ended abruptly during the reign of Arkamani-qo. When the priests sent word that Amun wished him dead, he "entered accompanied by some soldiers the shrine where was located the gold temple of the Aithiopians, and killed all the priests. After abolishing this custom, he reorganized affairs in accordance with his own plans."

Amenirdis, daughter of King Kashta, served as the wife of the god Amun.

Jebel Barkal

Overlooking the Kushite capital of Napata was Jebel Barkal. The Kushites believed the great god Amun lived inside this sacred mountain. A tall, pointed rock formation on one side of Jebel Barkal was said to be a cobra, ready to strike anyone who dared to harm the god inside. For centuries, the area was the most important religious center in Kush. Archaeologists have excavated the ruins of three palaces and thirteen temples at Jebel Barkal. The oldest surviving hieroglyphs were also discovered at the site.

These pyramids are some of the royal burial sites in Meroë.

Some scholars doubt Diodorus's story. But after Arkamani-qo's rule, the kings and queens of Kush were buried in Meroë, rather than at Jebel Barkal. If Arkamani-qo did in fact murder the priests at the Jebel Barkal temple, it is likely that rulers no longer felt it was a comfortable place to spend eternity.

Worshipping the Gods

At Jebel Barkal and other religious centers throughout Kush, priests worshipped a variety of gods and goddesses. Several of the most prominent, including Amun, Isis, and Osiris, were Egyptian deities introduced to Nubia before the rise of Kush. Their religious cults were probably revived during the period when the Kushite royals ruled Egypt as the pharaohs of the Twenty-Fifth Dynasty.

IMPORTANT KUSHITE GODS AND GODDESSES

NAME	DESCRIPTION	APPEARANCE
Amesemi	Goddess of protection and wife of Apedemak	Woman wearing a crown in the shape of a falcon, sometimes marked with a moon
Amun	God of the sun and creator of all things	Man with the head of a ram
Apedemak	Warrior god associated with the moon	Man with a lion's head, often holding weapons and wearing armor
Arensnuphis	God of life, air, and wind	Man with a feathered crown and a long skirt
Bastet	Goddess associated with motherhood	Cat or a woman with the head of a cat
Bes	Protector god of dancing and singing	Short, wide-faced man, often with the mane, tail, and ears of a lion
Hathor	Goddess of love and beauty who protected women during childbirth	Cow or a beautiful woman with a cow's ears and horns
Horus	Son of the Sun god Re and ancestor of all rulers	Falcon or a man with a falcon's head
Isis	Protector goddess of the dead associated with the hawk	Woman sitting on a throne, sometimes wearing a crown
Ma'at	Goddess of harmony and balance	Small woman with an ostrich feather on her head
Osiris	God associated with the afterlife and with dead rulers	Mummified man with a tall crown
Ptah	God of craftspeople and artists	Small man with a body covered with feathers
Sekhmet	Goddess of chaos and anger	Lion or a woman with the head of a lion
Taueret	Protector goddess of women	Hippopotamus with the tail of a crocodile and the paws of a lion
Thoth	God of the moon associated with language and wisdom	Bird or a man with a bird's head

Carved on the walls of Lion Temple in Naga, Sudan, this scene shows
Apedemak receiving an offering.

Most likely, these Kushite kings saw a political advantage in worshipping Egyptian gods and goddesses. Observing Egyptian religious customs and insisting that their power was mandated by Amun probably helped legitimize their rule in Egyptian eyes. Also, the Kushite kings perhaps sensed that forcing Kushite religious beliefs on Egypt might make their Egyptian subjects rebel.

Although the Kushites adopted many Egyptian religious customs, they tended to adapt them to fit in better with their own culture. For instance, in Kush, Amun was depicted in a number of ways, many designed to suit local tastes. The most important of these local forms was Amun of Napata. Although in Egypt Amun was depicted in human form, in Napata the god was given a ram's head.

The Kushites also felt comfortable worshipping older Nubian deities alongside those introduced from Egypt. The most important was the lion-headed god Apedemak. Throughout southern Kush, temples celebrated Apedemak as a war god. He was frequently shown holding a bow and arrows and slaying captives taken in battle. One temple inscription describes Apedemak as "one who sends forth a flaming breath against his enemies . . . [and] slays the rebels with [his] strength."

Temples and Graves

Kushite temple builders also employed both Nubian and Egyptian religious traditions. For temples dedicated to the worship of Apedemak, they usually constructed square, single-chambered, Nubian-style temples. For those of other gods, they often used a larger rectangular design that originated in Egypt. Each of these temples had a court, a hall for offerings, and a sanctuary surrounded by small chambers.

Temple Graffiti

Kushites who visited temples to pay homage to the gods often left behind graffiti, or writing carved into temple walls. The temple of Isis at Philae, for instance, is marked with graffiti written by Pasan, an envoy to Roman-held Egypt in the third century A.D. He made several trips from Meroë to Egypt, each time stopping at the temple to thank Isis for his safe passage. In one note, he wrote, "I am your good servant, Isis. . . . [M]y heart depends upon you in Egypt, in Meroë, and in the deserts."

The Egyptians influenced Kushite burial practices as well. The tombs of the rulers of Kush were marked with stone pyramids similar to those of the Egyptian pharaohs. The Kushites' pyramids were smaller, however. Also, in Kush pyramids were built on top of underground graves, whereas in Egypt bodies were buried in the pyramids themselves. For a time, Kush's kings were mummified before burial.

Like the Egyptians, the Kushites believed in a life after death. To make sure the dead had everything they needed in the afterlife, corpses were buried with a wide variety of goods. Archaeologists have found the most elaborate stashes of grave goods in the tombs of the wealthiest Kushites. Kings and queens were buried with jewelry, pottery, weapons, thumb rings, horse harnesses, wooden boxes, colored glass, and metal vessels. Many of these treasures were imported from ancient Egypt, Greece, and Rome.

Late in Kush history, *ba* statues were often buried with the dead. These stone figurines depicted humans with bird wings folded to their sides in the place of arms. The figures represented

These items, including some gold jewelry, were found in the tomb of King Aspelta.

Nuri

Between about 660 B.C. and 300 B.C., the kings of Kush were buried in tombs at Nuri. This burial site lies on the banks of the Nile a few miles upriver from Napata. While Nuri was in use, the kings' tombs were marked by stone pyramids. Long stairways led to the burial chambers beneath the pyramids. Once the corpse was inside, the stairways were filled with rubble to keep grave robbers out. The walls of the burial chambers were painted and carved with scenes and inscriptions that glorified the deceased rulers. Lying in coffins made of wood or stone, the bodies were mummified and their faces were covered with beautiful gold masks.

the ba, or the soul of the deceased. The wings allowed the soul to fly so it could join the sun god. The idea of the ba was Egyptian, but ba statues were unique to Kush. Like many Kushite sculptures, the ba statues have individualized facial features, creating minature portraits of the deceased.

Beginning with King Piankhy, many Kushite rulers adopted the Egyptian practice of placing *shabti* figures in their graves. The shabti were statues of humans, who would magically come to life to serve the ruler after his death. In Taharqa's tomb, there were more than one thousand shabti of various sizes made from alabaster, granite, and green ankerite stone.

Sacrifices to the Dead

In early Nubia, the rulers of the urban center of Kerma were buried with hundreds of other corpses. These people may have been servants of the rulers who were killed so they could continue serving their masters after death. It is also possible that they were prisoners taken in war and executed on the occasion of a ruler's death. Some kings of Kush were also buried with the bodies of human sacrifices, though generally with far fewer than Kerma's rulers were.

Slaughtered animals have also been found at the grave sites of several Kushite royals. At El-Kurru, archaeologists have excavated twenty-four horse graves, arranged in four parallel rows. Each row contained horses from the royal herds of a different king. Other Kushite graves included dogs, cattle, sheep, and even lions covered with jewelry.

With the deceased's happiness in the afterlife at stake, properly burying dead relatives was one of the Kushites' greatest responsibilities. In a funerary stele inscription, Piankhy-Kharuwt, the son of King Aspelta, expressed his gratitude to his father for his careful and generous burial: "You shall know these things which . . . Aspelta did for me: he built for me a pyramid of good white stone of the living rock; he provisioned for me a chapel of millions of years with every good thing."

This deceased person was buried in Kerma with a sacrificed servant and animal as well as food jars.

Chapter V

ARTISANS AND WRITERS

In 1834, an Italian doctor named Giuseppe Ferlini arrived in Nubia. He was determined to find some ancient art he could steal and then sell. Ferlini visited several Kushite burial sites but found that they had already been plundered. He then turned his attention to the pyramids in and around Meroë. With no concern for the proper preservation of these great monuments, the fortune hunter lopped off the top of one of the tallest.

Inside Ferlini found an unimaginable treasure, the jewelry of Queen Amanishakheto. Usually Kushite rulers stashed such goods in their underground burial chambers. For reasons unknown, Amanishakheto had instead placed her jewels in a chamber hidden near her pyramid's summit. Ironically, Ferlini's greed helped preserve these Kushite artifacts. After he sold them to several German princes, they ended up in European museums, where they are now preserved and displayed.

Grave goods such as Amanishakheto's provide one of the best sources of information about Kush. They offer clues about the lives and work of the artisans who made them.

They also offer clues about the ideas and beliefs that were important to all the Kushite people.

Flesh of the Gods

Amanishakheto's jewelry is both finely crafted and valuable, ornaments befitting a queen. Most of it was made of gold. Kushite craftspeople used the precious metal to make many beautiful objects, often decorated with glass or gems.

The Kushites also exported much of their gold. Traders sent shipments of gold down the Nile River into Egypt. From there, it was shipped and sold throughout the ancient world. Nubian gold was particularly prized by the Egyptians, who called the metal "the flesh of the gods." Many of the treasures found in the tombs of the pharaohs are made of gold imported from Nubia.

Mining gold was an extremely difficult task. In the second century B.C., when Egypt had gained control of gold deposits in northern Nubia, Greek historian Agatharchides of Cnidus wrote of the plight of the prisoners of war and convicted criminals

This bracelet is an excellent example of the handiwork of Kushite goldsmiths.

Naqa

The treasure of Queen Amanishakheto was discovered at Naqa. This site, located on the Nile about 40 miles (64 km) south of Meroë, included the ruins of the queen's huge palace. It was also a religious center that housed several temples. Recently, an archaeological team sponsored by the Egyptian Museum in Berlin, Germany, has made some amazing finds while excavating Naqa's Temple of Amun. Among the most notable are several well-preserved figurines of King Natakamani who, with his coruler Queen Amanitore, oversaw the temple's construction. Each figurine originally stood between the forelegs of a statue of a ram, an animal sacred to the Kushites.

forced to work in the mines: "[I]t is impossible for an observer to not pity the wretches because of the extremity of their suffering. For they meet with no respite at all, not the sick, the injured, the aged, not a woman by reason of her weakness, but all are compelled by blows to strive at their tasks until, exhausted by the abuse they suffered, they die in their miseries."

Borrowing Egyptian Traditions

As with so much of their culture, Kushite art displays a combination of several traditions. Most often, the artists of Kush borrowed techniques and decorative styles from the ancient Egyptians. During the Twenty-Fifth Dynasty, when Kush kings also ruled Egypt, Egyptian influences were especially prevalent in Kushite art. In fact, Kushite artists at that time revived several older Egyptian art styles, helping to initiate one of the greatest eras in the history of Egyptian art.

The kings of the Twenty-Fifth Dynasty certainly encouraged Kushite artists to look to Egyptian works for inspiration. They

Working Iron

In addition to being talented goldsmiths, Kushite artisans were also well known for their iron work. After mining metal-rich rock, they heated it in a furnace to melt the iron out and then hammered the iron into weapons and tools. Because Kushite craftspeople needed wood to fuel the fires in the furnaces, the city of Meroë, situated on the edge of a forest, became the kingdom's center of iron production.

In Kushite art, male figures have small heads in relation to their bodies as well as broad shoulders.

probably believed that ornaments, steles, temples, and monuments that looked Egyptian would helped legitimize their claims to the Egyptian throne. Some rulers even hired Egyptian craftspeople to design their art and architecture. King Taharqa, for instance, sent Egyptians to Kawa to build a temple dedicated to Amun.

On carvings on temple walls, Kushite artisans often copied figures and scenes directly from images on Egyptian temples. Artists throughout Kush probably knew these images from illustrated books. Therefore, the same scenes were carved by sculptors who lived centuries apart. Sometimes, the original meaning of an Egyptian scene was lost on Kushite artists. Drawing on a particularly popular design, one sculptor carved an image of a Kushite king or queen raising a club in one hand, preparing to kill a crowd of miniature-size enemies he or she was holding in the other. The picture was copied from an Egyptian scene in which the enemies were Kushites. In following the original too faithfully, the Kushite artist accidentally depicted the king killing his own subjects.

Most Kushite artisans, however, did not copy Egyptian art so blindly. Much of their work was guided by distinctly Kushite artistic traditions. For instance, their female figures have unusually wide hips, probably because Kushite artists were drawing on the older Nubian way of representing women. Male figures often have unusually broad shoulders and thick necks. And, unlike Egyptian artists, the Kushites frequently depicted humans with fairly realistic facial features. In many cases, the faces of Kushite figures seem to be modeled on the appearance of actual people.

Sculptures and Paintings

The Kushites who decorated the tombs and temples of their rulers were probably professional artists. They made freestanding sculptures, ranging from life-size shabti figures to small ba statues. They also carved into stone temple walls to create **reliefs**. In this type of sculpture, the area around the figures is cut away so that the figures appear to project slightly forward from the wall.

Reliefs most often show rulers and their families being presented to a procession of gods. But also common are sculptures showing rulers as warriors killing enemies of Kush. Other relief scenes depict war prisoners. One image at the site of Jebel Qeili shows prisoners falling down a mountainside, perhaps during a ceremonial execution.

Following the custom of most ancient artists of the time, Kushite sculptors painted their works in bright reds, yellows, and blues. However, the paint on most of these sculptures has long since worn away, so Kushite artworks in museums today appear to be made from bare, unpainted stone. The Kushites also decorated the exteriors of at least some temples and pyramids with paint. Late pyramids at Meroë were painted red and yellow, with a band of blue stars at the bottom.

Kushite artists also painted bare walls, though few of these paintings have survived. Creating wall paintings was probably an inexpensive alternative to carving reliefs. Even some fairly humble houses have painted walls. A wall painting in a house at Karanog, for instance, depicts a man on horseback fighting a variety of animals, including a camel and a crocodile. Some walls were painted white or colored with pink cement. On these neutral backgrounds, the Kushites hung weavings or wooden plaques painted with animal scenes.

Pottery

Generally, Kushite art was made for and used by the wealthy, either on earth or in the afterlife. One exception, however, was pottery, which archaeologists have found in the houses of common people. The earliest Kushite pots are unadorned, but later pottery made for everyday use is decorated.

A ceramic jar by a Kushite potter features two animal designs. At the top, there is a series of snakes, while giraffes circle the middle.

Some Kushite pottery was decorated with stamped designs, but more often it is painted. Some pots are adorned with geometric patterns. Others feature plant-inspired designs. Particularly popular is a vine pattern that was probably inspired by Greek art. Much of the best pottery painting depicts animals. Images of giraffes, antelopes, frogs, crocodiles, snakes, and birds are frequently found on Kushite pots.

Although common subjects for temple art, the gods generally do not appear on Kushite pottery. Perhaps the Kushites considered it inappropriate to paint such sacred images on utilitarian objects. On some pots, however, human beings are pictured. Most are herdspeople, shown looking after cattle. A few rare pots depict violent scenes of war prisoners and of people being eaten by large animals.

The pottery produced by late Kushite artists was among the finest in the ancient world. Especially prized was eggshell ware. The sides of these pots are extremely thin. These vessels had no practical use, but were coveted as luxury goods. They were probably valued as status symbols by the Kushite elite.

Writing in Meroitic

Another notable artistic tradition of the Kushites is the art of writing. For hundreds of years, the Kushites used Egyptian hieroglyphic writing to record tomb and temple inscriptions. These texts were probably carved by priests who had learned to read and write the Egyptian script or by Egyptian scribes brought to Kush to carve inscriptions.

By about the second century B.C., however, the Kushites developed their own writing system, now known as Meroitic. It was probably used to record a local language spoken by average Kushites. The ancient Greek historian Diodorus claimed all

This tablet shows a cursive version of Meroitic.

the Kushites knew how to write in their own script, but in fact very few probably did. More likely, the script was known only by the elites, since it was used primarily to write important texts on behalf of Kushite royals and to mark the tombstones of the wealthy.

The Rosetta Stone

In 1799, French soldiers made an amazing discovery near the city of Rosetta in northern Egypt. It was a stone slab dating from the reign of Egyptian pharaoh Ptolemy V (205 B.C.–180 B.C.). The stone was inscribed with the same message in several languages, including Egyptian hieroglyphics and ancient Greek. The Rosetta Stone provided the key modern scholars needed to decipher hieroglyphic writing. Archaeologists today are searching for a similar stone inscribed with Meroitic and a known ancient script to help scholars at last understand the Kushites' writings.

The first Meroitic inscriptions used an alphabet derived from Egyptian glyphs, or picture signs. The glyphs were usually written in columns, as Egyptian hieroglyphs were. But unlike hieroglyphs, in which most pictures stood for complete words, Meroitic used twenty-three glyphs to represent different sounds. The parts of each word were separated by two or three dots. Eventually, the Kushites simplified the Meroitic glyphs into cursive versions. Meroitic cursive is found on some pottery and may have also been used to write on papyrus.

While scholars are still not able to read Meroitic, they have been able to identify some personal and place names. They also know what sounds were represented by each letter. As the study of Kush continues, it is certainly possible that, one day, all the secrets of Meroitic writing will be unlocked, revealing an entirely new perspective on the Kushite world.

Chapter VI

THE COMMON PEOPLE

In temples and tombs, the Kushites left behind dozens of images of their kings and queens and other elites of Kushite society. But few artists depicted Kush's average citizens. These were the common people who struggled to eke out a living in their kingdom's punishing environment.

Only recently have archaeologists begun to look for clues about how Kushite commoners lived. In addition to this growing body of information, there are a few comments about average Kushites recorded by ancient writers. For several of these historians, the most outstanding characteristic of Kush's common people was their strong religious faith and moral sense. In the first century A.D., Nicolaus of Damascus wrote, "They cultivate piety and righteousness. Their houses have no doors; and although there are many things left lying in the streets, no one ever steals them."

The Kushite People

A few writers in Greece and Rome were struck by the Kushites' physical appearance. According to the historian Diodorus, they had dark skin, flat noses, and woolly hair. The Roman scholar Pliny theorized that their appearance was due to the

A sculpture depicts an ancient Kushite with traditional features.

Women wore a type of ancient makeup called kohl to create lines around their eyes.

hot climate of Kush: "[T]here is no doubt that the Aithiopians [Kushites] are scorched by the heat through their closeness to the sun; they have a burnt appearance when they are born, and their beards and hair are curly."

Diodorus also wrote about the clothing of the common Kushites. He noted that, in the heat, "some do not wear clothes at all, going about always naked." Sometimes, however, the Kushites wore "the skins of domesticated animals, and some cover their bodies to the waist with aprons woven from hair." Archaeologists have found a variety of clothing at Kushite sites, including tunics, loincloths, and belts.

Though much of the time, Kushites probably went barefoot, both commoners and elites sometimes wore sandals. The wealthy wore footwear made from colored leather that was decorated with stamped designs. The sandals of commoners were much less fancy. They were generally made from plant materials, most commonly palms.

Archaeologists have found jewelry in even the humblest graves. Both men and women wore earrings, necklaces, and anklets. Kushite women also adorned their fingernails and hair with henna, a dye made from ground plants. In addition, they used kohl, a dark powder that was mixed with liquid, to paint their eyelids. Artisans made elaborate decorated tubes out of wood and ivory to store this cosmetic.

In Kushite art, women are often depicted as heavy, with particularly broad hips. Extra weight on women was likely considered a sign of both beauty and high social status. Common women probably did not have enough extra food to achieve this look.

Farming in Kush

Average Kushites made their living off the land. Most were farmers, who also raised a few animals to add to their food supply. Farming in Kush was difficult. In Egypt, the Nile overflowed its banks each year, leaving behind a layer of fertile silt. But in Kush, the banks of the Nile were so high they prevented this beneficial flooding. The land of Kush, therefore, was far less rich than that of its northern neighbor. Also, Kushite farmers were at the mercy of changing rates of rainfall. A slight fluctuation in the number of rainy days could destroy an otherwise healthy crop.

Some Kushite farmers used a simple device to irrigate their lands. Known as a *haqia*, it featured a vertical wooden wheel that, when turned, moved loops of ropes to which pots were attached.

A modern illustration shows how a haqia might have worked in ancient times.

Dipped in the river, the pots were filled with water, then raised high above the banks, where the water was dumped into a canal and diverted to the fields. The haqia was especially useful in northern Kush, where there was relatively little rainfall. But even there, the amount of land a farmer could irrigate with a haqia was fairly small.

Sorghum was perhaps the most important food crop for Kushite farmers. This grass, which is native to Africa, probably grew wild in Nubia before farmers learned how to cultivate it. Sorghum is celebrated in several Kushite artworks. On a wall of a temple at Naqa, the god Apedemak is shown offering a bundle of this valuable plant food.

Other crops the Kushites may have grown include barley, beans, and lentils, which would have provided them with needed protein. Several ancient sources claim they grew cotton. The Kushites may have woven cotton into cloth for export to Egypt. There, cotton clothing was commonly worn by priests. The Kushites also grew groves of date palms. These trees provided sweet dates as well as palm leaves, which were used as clothing and building materials.

Animal Herders

Although famed for their skill with bows and arrows, common Kushites rarely hunted for food. The wealthy, however, possibly hunted for sport, stalking such large prey as lions and rhinoceroses. Fish bones and jars for fish sauce have been found at some sites, but the Kushites apparently fished fairly little. They might have considered eating fish a violation of their religious beliefs. One tomb inscription notes that eating fish is "an abomination to the house of the king."

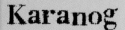

Karanog

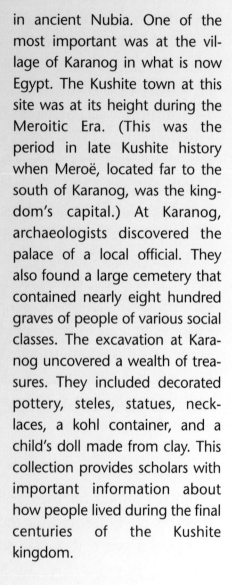

Between 1907 and 1910, an archaeological expedition from the University Museum of Philadelphia studied several sites in ancient Nubia. One of the most important was at the village of Karanog in what is now Egypt. The Kushite town at this site was at its height during the Meroitic Era. (This was the period in late Kushite history when Meroë, located far to the south of Karanog, was the kingdom's capital.) At Karanog, archaeologists discovered the palace of a local official. They also found a large cemetery that contained nearly eight hundred graves of people of various social classes. The excavation at Karanog uncovered a wealth of treasures. They included decorated pottery, steles, statues, necklaces, a kohl container, and a child's doll made from clay. This collection provides scholars with important information about how people lived during the final centuries of the Kushite kingdom.

The Kushites, however, did keep herds of domesticated animals. Most important of these were cattle. They often appear walking in procession in Kushite reliefs. The Kushites also kept sheep, goats, and horses.

The tribes that occupied the desert lands near Kushite settlements were also animal herders. Agatharchides of Cnidus claimed that the men of these desert people were so diligent in the care of

Images of cattle can be found on many Kushite works of art because these animals were greatly valued.

their animals that they never slept: "They possess a large number of animals which accompany them, and they hang cowbells from the horns of all the males in order that their sound might drive off wild beasts. At nightfall, they collect their herds into [barns] and cover these with hurdles made from palm branches. Their women and children mount up on top of these. The men, however, light fires in a circle and sing traditional tales and thus ward off sleep."

Cattle and sheep were so crucial to the desert tribes' survival that they often battled each other for control over their pasture lands. According to Agatharchides, "When summer comes, . . . they live in the marshlands, fighting among themselves over the pasture. . . . In their feuds, they first pelt each other with stones until some are wounded." Especially in southern Kush, these desert peoples posed a constant threat to Kushite farmers. They often raided Kushite settlements, making off with food and animals.

Everyday Life Among the Kushites
Aside from their food-getting activities, little is known about the life of Kushite commoners. Scholars and archaeologists, however, have unearthed a few details about other aspects of their day-to-day existence.

In comparison with the royal palaces, the houses of the average Kushites were simple structures. As the Greek writer Strabo wrote, "In the towns the dwellings are made of material split from palm trees, plaited [reeds or palm leaves] for walls, [as well as] of bricks." These bricks were made from mud and dried in kilns.

The kilns used to bake mud bricks were also used to fire pottery. Most household pottery was probably molded by hand by women. Some pots were unadorned, but others, even a few made for everyday use, were carefully formed and beautifully decorated with paint and stamped designs. Women were also weavers who used looms to create cloth and decorative textiles at home.

At some Kushite sites, archaeologists have found imported **amphorae**, two-handled jugs used to hold wine. The Kushites probably grew their own grapes and stamped them with their feet to make this beverage. One building at the site of Qasr Ibrim

Many of the common people lived in simple homes in villages. Archaeologists discovered one such village called Ash-Shaukan, shown here.

A wall carving shows two dancers performing. It is thought that dancing may
have been a form of entertainment as well as an expression of religious devotion.

appears to have been a tavern. Its six rooms were filled with amphorae and goblets. One wall was adorned with a carved image of grapes.

A number of wall and pottery paintings show Kushite dancers. Dances were part of Kushite religious ceremonies, but dancing may have been also a form of entertainment. The Kushites certainly made and played a variety of musical instruments. In Kushite sites, archaeologists have found numerous drums and flutes, which were possibly imported from Greece or Egypt. At the temple of Kawa, one wall depicts musicians playing drums, horns, and harps, suggesting that, despite their often difficult lives, the Kushites still enjoyed moments of joy.

Chapter VII

THE END OF KUSH

"And I came to Kasu [Kush] and I fought a battle and made prisoners of its people. . . . And the day after I arrived I sent [armies] out to raid the country . . . and the cities built of bricks and those of reeds. . . . [My armies] killed, and captured prisoners and cast people into the water."

With these words, recorded in a tomb inscription, Ezana, the king of Aksum, celebrated his brutal attack on the Kushite capital of Meroë in about A.D. 360. The Aksumites' invasion was a hard blow, from which Kush never recovered. But the end of Kush did not result from just one event. Scholars now believe the kingdom's decline happened over a period of time for a variety of reasons.

Trade Along the Red Sea

For one thousand years, Kush relied on trade for much of its wealth. Because the kingdom controlled the southern reaches of the Nile River, the Kushites became successful middlemen in the trade that brought products from central Africa down to prosperous Egypt.

Beginning in the third century A.D., this lucrative trade route was becoming obsolete. Egypt had less power and less

The stele was built to honor King Ezana. He was king of Aksum, a kingdom that neighbored Kush and thrived while Kush declined.

wealth, greatly reducing its demand for the exports offered by Kushite traders. At the same time, another trade route opened up. It brought goods from the interior of Africa to Egypt and the Middle East by way of the Red Sea. This route went through the rising kingdom of Aksum, located to the east of Kush in what is now Ethiopia. As the Red Sea trade increased, Aksum grew richer while Kush grew poorer. Evidence of Kush's increasing poverty comes from royal burial sites. After the first century A.D., kings' tombs and tomb monuments were smaller and made from cheaper materials.

King Ezana of Aksum was particularly effective at exploiting the new Red Sea trade route. He was a convert to Christianity, which helped him foster a good relationship with the Romans, also Christians, who at that time controlled Egypt. Ezana was also brutal in punishing anyone who threatened his traders. An inscription describes a war Ezana waged on the kingdom of Afan, after its people attacked an Aksumite trade caravan: "[A] slaughter took place, of the men of Afan 503, and women 202, in all 705. . . . [Prisoners were taken], men 40, and women and children 165, in all 205. As spoil were carried off 31,900 and 57 cattle, baggage animals, 827."

Invaders Strike

While dealing with economic troubles because of the Red Sea trade, the Kushites also faced a new threat from neighboring desert tribes. For hundreds of years, desert peoples had raided Kushite settlements from time to time. In the past, the Kushites had been able to repel these attacks. But by the fourth century A.D., holding back the belligerent desert tribes became harder. These people may have acquired camels, making them a more mobile, and therefore more effective, fighting force.

Ballana and Qustul

During the 1930s, archaeologists began unearthing the sites of Ballana and Qustul from the post-Kush era. There, they found the tombs of kings and nobles of the kingdom of Nobatia. By this time, the elites of Nubia were no longer buried under pyramids. Instead, their tombs were topped by giant mounds. The tomb chambers were filled with food, weapons, and tools. Several skeletons wore elaborate silver crowns inlaid with jewels, indicating that these people were likely rulers. Many tombs contained the bodies of human and animal sacrifices. This practice, dating from the Kerma period, suggests a continuity in ancient Nubian burial customs that outlasted the fall of Kush.

In addition, the Kushites' financial woes may have left them ill equipped to battle these old enemies. Archaeologists have found several Kushite forts that were possibly built during this period. Their presence suggests that the Kushite kings were trying to respond to increased aggression from the desert tribes. But even with this effort, it is possible that the kings simply no longer had enough wealth to support the large army needed to wage a decisive war against their tribal enemies.

The desert tribes were probably taking over Kushite territory just as the kingdom of Aksum began expanding to the west. By the time Ezana's armies arrived in Meroë, the city may already have been taken over by foreign nomads. Probably, Ezana was aware that Kush was falling to its desert attackers. By invading Meroë, the king of Aksum could take advantage of Kush's weakness and eliminate an important trade rival once and for all.

Overtaken by enemies and poverty, the kingdom of Kush fell apart. But as some scholars have pointed out, its demise is less surprising than the fact that Kush existed for as long as it did. The cataracts of the Nile River made travel through the Kushite territory difficult. Given its geography, Kush was not a likely place for a single, unified state to thrive. Somewhat amazingly, the rulers of Kush were able to hold together a prosperous kingdom despite this obstacle for more than one thousand years.

Remnants of Kushite Culture

By about A.D. 400, three new kingdoms—Alwa, Makuria, and Nobatia—had emerged in the lands that had been Kush. These states had fewer urban areas than did Kush. But people still gathered in some organized settlements big enough to be called towns.

Any remaining elements of Kushite culture were abandoned after the Roman emperor Justinian I introduced Christianity to the region.

The people of these kingdoms also continued to observe some Kushite ways. Some artifacts made by them feature Kushite symbols. Much of their pottery was cruder than that crafted during the Kushite era. But some particularly well made pottery indicates that the artisans of these later kingdoms retained some Kushite artistic traditions. Archaeological evidence also suggests that these peoples continued to worship at least some of the Kushite gods.

In the mid-sixth century A.D., however, the remnants of Kushite culture were suddenly abandoned as the Christian religion was introduced to Nubia. Justinian I, the emperor of Christianized Rome, sent missionaries to Africa to convert the Nubians. Church historian John of Ephesus wrote of one Roman missionary's work there: "[T]he blessed Julian . . . remained with them for two years, though suffering greatly from the extreme heat. . . . Nevertheless, he endured it patiently, and taught them, and baptized both the king and nobles, and [many] people also."

Once Nubia's rulers became Christian, the new religion spread rapidly among the people of the region. With the conversion of the Nubians, the Kushite religion was forgotten. Old Kushite ways also became things of the past.

The Emergence of Sudan

Within a century of Nubia's conversion, it was threatened with non-Christian enemies to the north. Egypt, then part of the Byzantine Empire, was taken over by Islamic Arabs in 642. The Arabs also invaded Nubia, but they were soundly defeated at the Makurian capital of Dongola. A peace treaty made with the Arabs preserved Nubian independence.

Muhammad-Ali built his own empire in the lands that once belonged to the Kushites.

The Nubian kingdoms remained Christian until about 1500. At about this time, the kings of Funj, located to the south,

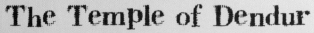

The Temple of Dendur

The Temple of Dendur, located in the Metropolitan Museum of Art in New York City, is an extraordinary artifact of ancient Kush. The temple was built in northern Kush in about 15 B.C. by the Roman emperor Augustus, who then ruled over Egypt. A shrine to the goddess Isis, the temple was dismantled in 1963 before it would be destroyed by the construction of the Aswan Dam. In 1965, the pieces of the temple, weighing more than 800 tons, were shipped to the museum, where the temple was rebuilt.

extended their rule into Nubia and helped spread Islam through the region. During the next three hundred years, the kingdoms of Nubia broke up into numerous small Islamic states.

By the nineteenth century, Nubia was known as the Sudan, meaning "land of the blacks" in Arabic. In 1820, Muhammad-Ali sent an army from Egypt into the Sudan and founded the city of Khartoum. Muhammad-Ali continued to extend his kingdom, and ultimately built the largest empire ever known in central Africa.

By the mid-nineteenth century, Europeans began arriving in Nubia. Some were explorers. Others were archaeologists. Still others were soldiers from the British army. In 1898, these Englishmen helped Egypt take control of the Sudan. The region remained under English rule until 1956, when it became an independent state officially known as the Republic of the Sudan. Since then, the land that was Kush has been part of two modern African nations, Egypt and Sudan.

Kush Today

In the nineteenth century, the serious study of Kush began as archaeologists started excavating Nubian sites. Still, Egypt attracted the attention of most students of ancient Africa. Important sites such as Kerma, Napata, and Meroë were not fully excavated until the early twentieth century.

The field of Nubiology, however, was not truly born until even later. The event that triggered worldwide interest in Nubia was the expansion of the Aswan Dam. In 1961, Egypt began work on this massive dam on the Nile River in order to control flooding and produce electricity. When completed, the dam would create an enormous lake that would cover what had been northern Kush. If the sites in the region were not excavated quickly, all the

Archaeologists continue to search for and discover new Kushite sites. Here, an archaeologist records the location of walls in an ancient Kushite home.

artifacts and other information they contained would be lost forever.

Archaeologists around the world responded. More than forty archaeological teams rushed to Egypt. For eight years, they worked to uncover the remains of ancient Nubia, exploring numerous sites along a 300-mile (483-km) stretch of the Nile. Because of their efforts, thousands of Nubian objects are preserved in museums across the globe.

These excavations also inspired more scholars to study southern Nubia, whose lands are now part of Sudan. The Sudanese government has supported archaeological digs in the country. But unfortunately, a raging civil war has made it dangerous for archaeologists to work there. Also threatening further study is development in the region. The construction of new dams, bridges, highways, and irrigation projects could destroy sites that have not yet been excavated.

With so much still unknown, Nubiology is one of the most exciting areas of study in modern archaeology. Today's archaeologists are still finding new Kushite artifacts, while researchers continue the struggle to decipher Meroitic writings. As a result, the story of Kush is best regarded as a work in progress. Our understanding of this story is sure to change and grow as this ancient land comes more fully into focus.

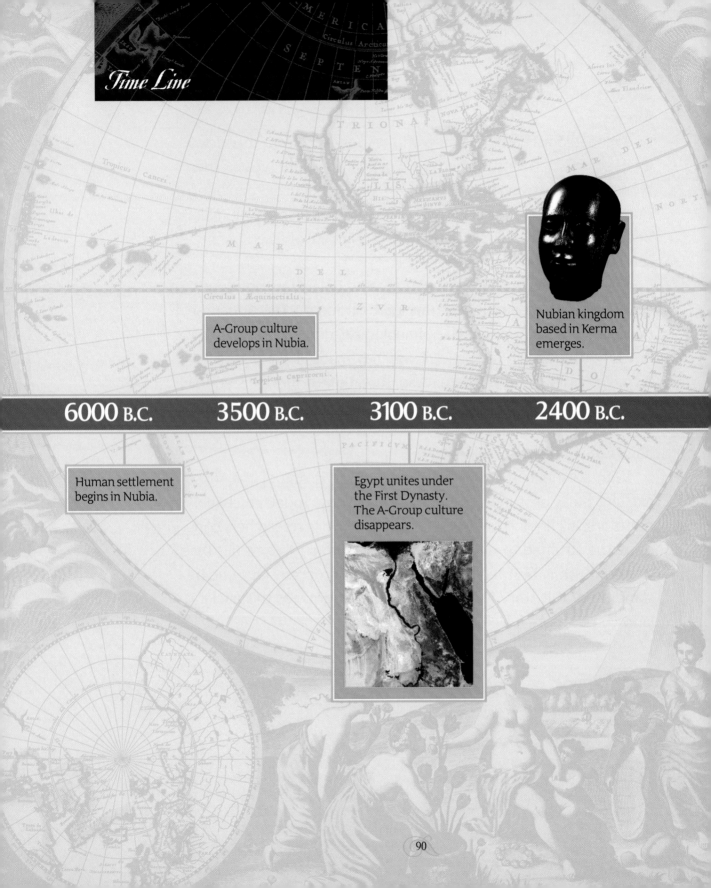

A-Group culture develops in Nubia.

Nubian kingdom based in Kerma emerges.

| 6000 B.C. | 3500 B.C. | 3100 B.C. | 2400 B.C. |

Human settlement begins in Nubia.

Egypt unites under the First Dynasty. The A-Group culture disappears.

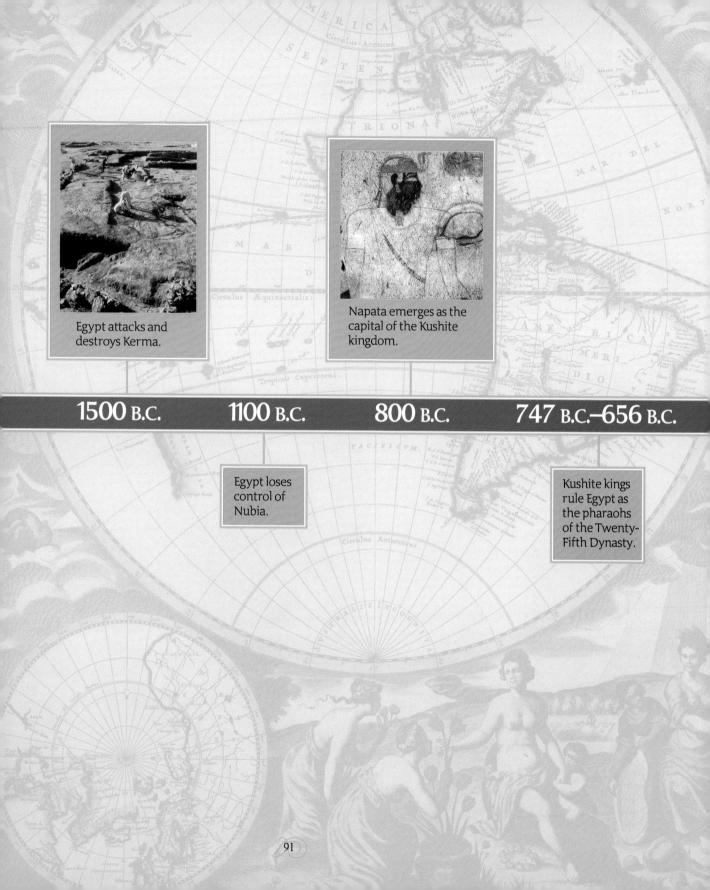

Egypt attacks and
destroys Kerma.

Napata emerges as the
capital of the Kushite
kingdom.

| 1500 B.C. | 1100 B.C. | 800 B.C. | 747 B.C.–656 B.C. |

Egypt loses
control of
Nubia.

Kushite kings
rule Egypt as
the pharaohs
of the Twenty-
Fifth Dynasty.

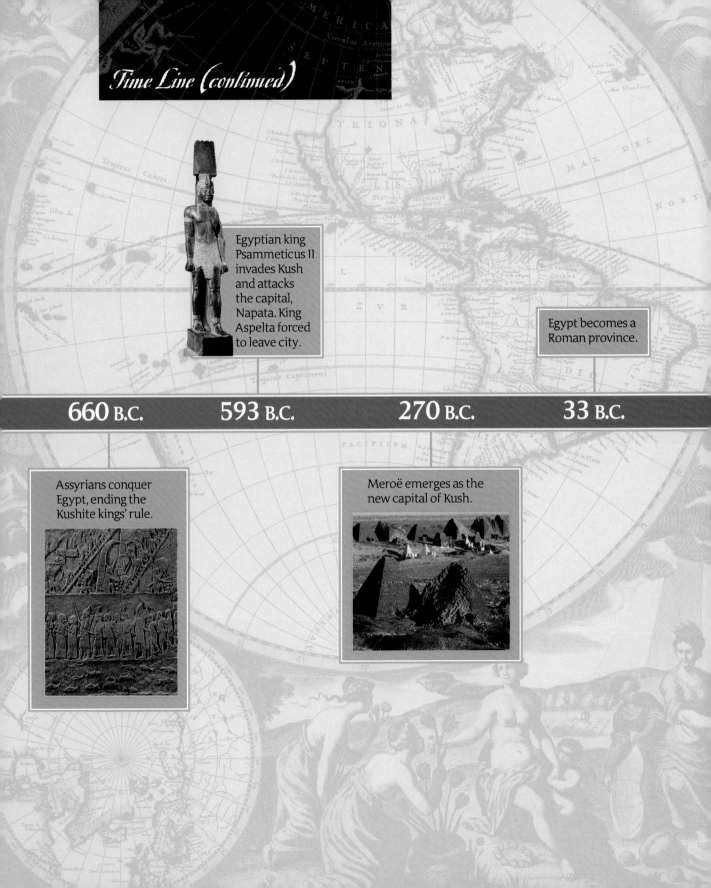

Time Line (continued)

Egyptian king Psammeticus II invades Kush and attacks the capital, Napata. King Aspelta forced to leave city.

Egypt becomes a Roman province.

660 B.C. **593 B.C.** **270 B.C.** **33 B.C.**

Assyrians conquer Egypt, ending the Kushite kings' rule.

Meroë emerges as the new capital of Kush.

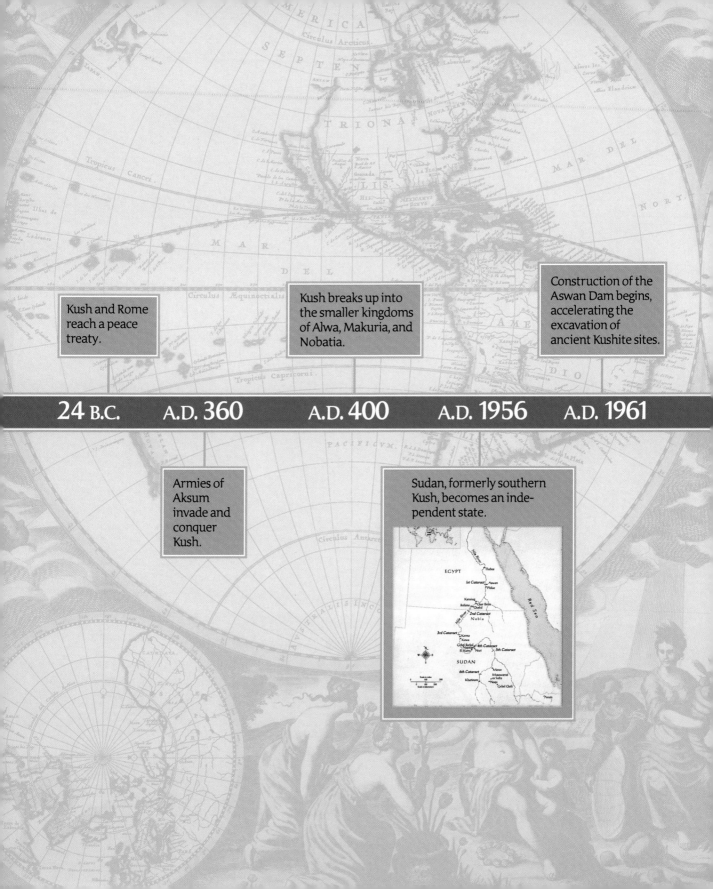

Kush and Rome
reach a peace
treaty.

Kush breaks up into
the smaller kingdoms
of Alwa, Makuria, and
Nobatia.

Construction of the
Aswan Dam begins,
accelerating the
excavation of
ancient Kushite sites.

24 B.C.   **A.D. 360**   **A.D. 400**   **A.D. 1956**   **A.D. 1961**

Armies of
Aksum
invade and
conquer
Kush.

Sudan, formerly southern
Kush, becomes an inde-
pendent state.

Amenirdis

The daughter of the Kushite king Kashta, Amenirdis joined her brother Piankhy in Egypt in about 740 B.C. After succeeding Kashta, Piankhy conquered Egypt and became the first pharaoh of the Twenty-Fifth Dynasty. At the religious center of Thebes, Amenirdis was declared the wife of Amun, the patron god of both Egypt and Kush. Amenirdis helped rule Egypt during the kingships of Piankhy, her other brother Shabaqo, and her two nephews Shebitqo and Taharqa.

Aspelta

Ruled 600 B.C.–580 B.C.

During his reign, Kushite king Aspelta attempted to fend off an Egyptian army led by the pharaoh Psammeticus II. The Egyptian force made its way to the Kushite capital of Napata, forcing Aspelta to relocate his court to Meroë. He was buried in a pyramid tomb at Nuri. Excavations there have uncovered many beautiful Kushite objects made from alabaster and gold.

Harsiotef

Ruled 390 B.C.–350 B.C.

Harsiotef ruled Kush longer than any other king or queen. A stele inscribed with Egyptian hieroglyphs found at Jebel Barkal describes his reign. Throughout his kingship, Harsiotef battled nomadic peoples from the desert lands near Kush. According to the stele, these enemies once took over Meroë, the Kushite capital. Harsiotef also launched several military campaigns to the north in an effort to expand Kush.

Irike-amanote

Ruled 430 B.C.–400 B.C.

Irike-amanote distinguished himself as a warrior king. As soon as he was chosen for the kingship, he sent warriors to battle against rebelling nomads near Meroë. He later put down another revolt in the north. During this conflict, he took many captives whom he put to work as servants in Kushite temples. Irike-amanote may have also provided warriors to the Egyptians as they fought off invaders from Persia.

Kashta

Ruled 760 B.C.–747 B.C.

Kashta was probably the brother of Alara, the earliest known ruler of Kush. Kashta tried to expand Kush to the north. During his rule, Kush took control of lands south of Aswan.

Nastasen

Ruled 335 B.C.–315 B.C.

Nastasen's reign as king of Kush is described on a stele from Jebel Barkal. Soon after he became king, an Egyptian leader—equipped with ships, an army, and a huge herd of cattle—invaded Kush. Nastasen turned the tables, attacking and defeating the invaders and making off with their goods as war booty. He also successfully fought several nomadic tribes, taking a great number of enemies as captives.

Natakamani and Amanitore

Ruled A.D. 1–A.D. 20

Among the last rulers of Kush were Natakamani and Amanitore. Husband and wife, they shared power during their twenty-year joint rule. They sponsored numerous building projects, which were often adorned with their images. The most famous appears on a wall of a temple at Naqa in present-day Sudan. The god Apedemak is pictured in the center with Natakamani and Amanitore, in identical poses, standing to his left and right.

Piankhy

Ruled 747 B.C.–716 B.C.

Piankhy, also known as Piye, was king of Kush. Soon after his coronation, he invaded Egypt. After a second attack, the princes of Egypt surrendered to his forces. Piankhy returned to the Kushite capital of Napata, from which he continued to rule over both Kush and Egypt. Much of his reign was devoted to rebuilding the religious complex at Jebel Barkal.

Shabaqo

Ruled 716 B.C.–702 B.C.

Succeeding his brother Piankhy, Shabaqo was the second king of Kush to rule Egypt as well. During his reign, Kush's control over Egypt was threatened when a group of Egyptian princes rebelled. Shabaqo reconquered Egypt and then moved there in order to keep a tighter rein over the region. The first Kushite king to live in Egypt, Shabaqo returned to Kush only after death. His mummified body was buried in the royal cemetery at el-Kurru in present-day Sudan.

Shebitqo

Ruled 702 B.C.–690 B.C.

He was one of the Kushite kings of Egypt's Twenty-Fifth Dynasty. Shebitqo nearly lost the Kushite empire to the Assyrians from what is now northern Iraq. To prevent the Assyrian army's advance toward Egypt, Shebitqo joined forces with the kings of Israel and placed Taharqa (probably his brother) in charge of reinforcements from Kush. The combined forces, along with a plague, compelled the Assyrians to retreat.

Taharqa

Ruled 690 B.C.–664 B.C.

Before ascending the throne of Kush, Taharqa was famous for his battlefield exploits. At twenty, Taharqa led the Kush army against Assyrian forces that threatened Egypt's borders. Taharqa ruled following the death of King Shebitqo, who was probably his brother. Taharqa initiated many new building projects, including the construction of several temples. Later in his reign, Taharqa was plagued by repeated Assyrian attacks. As the Assyrian army advanced, Taharqa was forced to flee to Napata, where he died. His tomb was topped by a 150-foot (45.7-m) high pyramid, the tallest one built in what is now Sudan.

Tanwetamani

Ruled 664 B.C.–653 B.C.

Tanwetamani was the nephew of Taharqa. Soon after he became king, his forces rushed into Egypt and reclaimed it for Kush. Tanwetamani held Egypt for less than two years. The Assyrian king sent an army to Egypt, which succeeded in driving Tanwetamani's warriors out. Tanwetamani escaped and remained the king of Kush until his death. He was the last Kushite king to rule Egypt.

amphorae two-handled jugs used to hold wine

archaeology the study of cultures based on material objects people leave behind

artifact an object, such as a weapon, tool, or ornament, used to study a past culture

ba a dead person's soul, according to the ancient Kushites and Egyptians

cataract an area along a river where rocks and islands create rapids in the water

diorite a precious dark blue stone found in Nubia

dynasty a succession of rulers from the same family

excavation the systematic digging up of an archaeological site to uncover the remains of a culture

haqia a device the Kushites used to irrigate dry land

hieroglyphs a system of picture writing, like the one used by the ancient Egyptians and briefly adopted by the Kushites

inscription words or pictures cut into a stone surface, such as a stele or wall

Kush kingdom that ruled lands in what is now Egypt and Sudan between 800 B.C. and A.D. 350

Meroitic writing system used by the Kushites from about 180 B.C. to A.D. 400

militia an army made up of ordinary citizens instead of professional soldiers

nomad a member of a group that moves from place to place with the seasons in search of sources of food and water

Nubia a geographic area south of ancient Egypt that included lands in what are now southern Egypt and northern Sudan

piety extreme religious devotion and sense of duty

pike a long spear

relief a sculpture created by carving away the background of a flat surface, making sculpted figures and objects seem to project forward

shabti human-shaped figurines buried with some Kushite rulers in order to serve them in the afterlife

sorghum a type of grass that can be used to make a sweet syrup

stele a rectangular slab of stone inscribed with writing or art and used as a monument

uraei sacred serpents used to represent kingship in Kushite art and costume

Books

Bianchi, Robert Steven. *The Nubians: People of the Ancient Nile.* Brookfield, CT: Millbrook Press, 1994.

Haynes, Joyce L. *Nubia: Ancient Kingdoms of Africa.* Boston: Museum of Fine Arts, 1992.

Levy, Patricia Marjorie. *Sudan.* New York: Benchmark Books, 1997.

Mann, Kenny. *African Kingdoms of the Past: Egypt, Kush, Aksum.* Parsippany, NJ: Dillon Press, 1997.

Panchyk, Richard. *Archaeology for Kids: Uncovering the Mysteries of Our Past.* Chicago: Chicago Review Press, 2001.

Russmann, Edna R. *Nubian Kingdoms.* New York: Franklin Watts, 1998.

Service, Pamela F. *The Ancient African Kingdom of Kush.* New York: Benchmark Books, 1998.

Organizations and Online Sites

Ancient Nubia: Egypt's Rival in Africa
http://www.umich.edu/~kelseydb/Exhibits/AncientNubia/

Sponsored by the Kelsey Museum of Archaeology, this site includes photographs from the Nubian art collection of Philadelphia's University Museum and a history of the Aswan Dam's effect on Nubian archaeology.

Black Kingdoms of the Nile
http://www.pbs.org/wonders/

This is the companion site to an episode of the Public Broadcasting System's series "Wonders of the African World." It includes short essays about various aspects of ancient Nubia and video footage of modern Sudan.

Dig Nubia
http://www.dignubia.org

Full of fascinating information, this Web site is based on a traveling museum exhibition. It includes an extensive time line, biographies of Nubian rulers, illustrations and descriptions of important artifacts, and many other resources for students and teachers.

Egypt: A New Look @ an Ancient Culture
http://www.museum.upenn.edu/new/exhibits/online_exhibits/egypt/nubia.shtml

This virtual exhibition explores the Egyptian collections at the University Museum at the University of Pennsylvania, but also includes some information on the museum's Nubian artifacts.

Explore Ancient Egypt
http://www.mfa.org/egypt/explore_ancient_egypt/

Boston's Museum of Fine Arts has one of the finest collections of Nubian and Egyptian art in the United States. Its virtual exhibition "Explore Ancient Egypt" describes the archaeological expeditions that brought these objects to the museum.

The Nubia Salvage Project
http://oi.uchicago.edu/OI/PROJ/NUB/Nubia.html

This site, put together by the University of Chicago's Oriental Institute, discusses the efforts to salvage Nubian archaeological sites in the 1960s and includes the text of brochures written for two of the museum's exhibitions of Nubian artifacts.

Nubianet
http://www.nubianet.org

This site offers a brief history of Nubia, including a helpful collection of quotations from ancient and modern writers. In a section of Web pages geared especially for kids, it also provides a guide for students interested in a career in archaeology.

Sudan Page: African Studies Center, University of Pennsylvania
http://www.sas.upenn.edu/African_Studies/Country_Specific/
Sudan.html .

This page offers basic facts about Sudan and a variety of links to sites dealing with Sudan's past and present.

About the Author

Liz Sonneborn is a writer, living in Brooklyn, New York. A graduate of Swarthmore College, she has written more than forty books for children and adults, including *The American West, A to Z of American Women in the Performing Arts*, and *The New York Public Library's Amazing Native American History*, winner of a 2000 Parent's Choice Award.